This book belongs to:

_____

_____

CROSS STITCH PATTERNS FROM 1800 Vol. 1

Compiled by Angela M. Foster

You are welcome to use any of the <u>designs</u> in this book <u>to make things for</u> personal uses, charities, and selling.

ISBN 13 -   978-1542464147
ISBN 10 -   1542464145

Copyrighted © 2017 by Angela M. Foster
All Rights Reserved.

I dedicate this book to

all who love to use their hands

to make beautiful items.

All of the designs in this book were created by

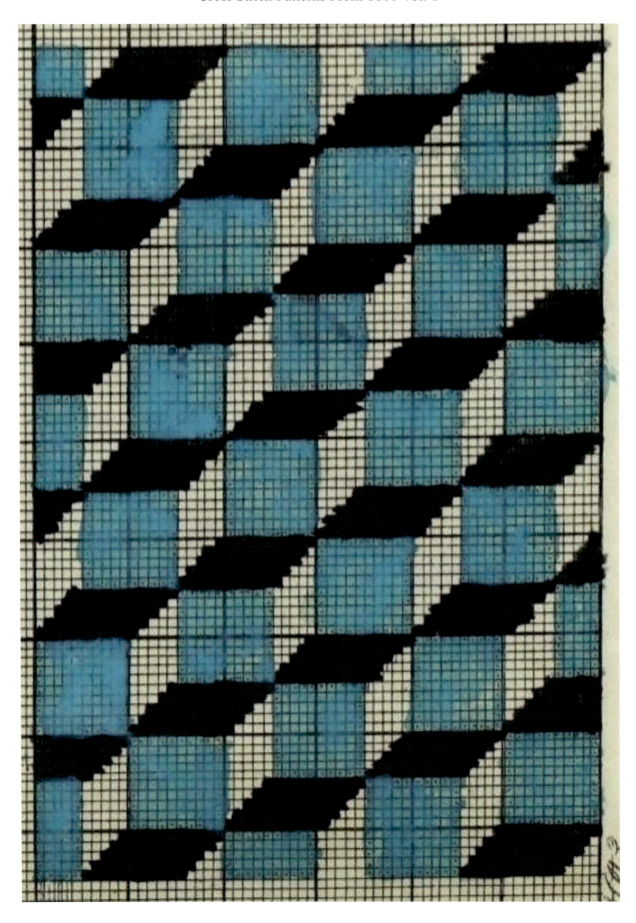

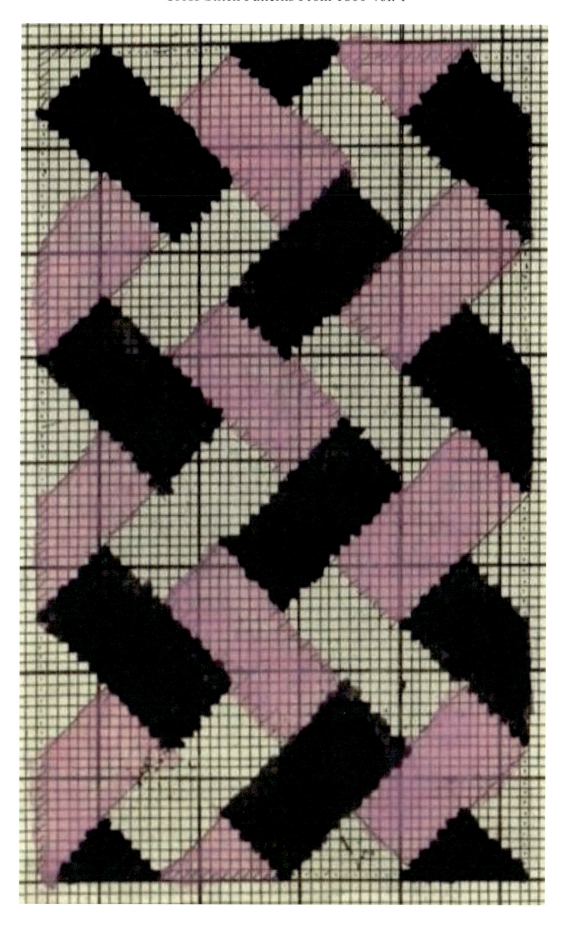

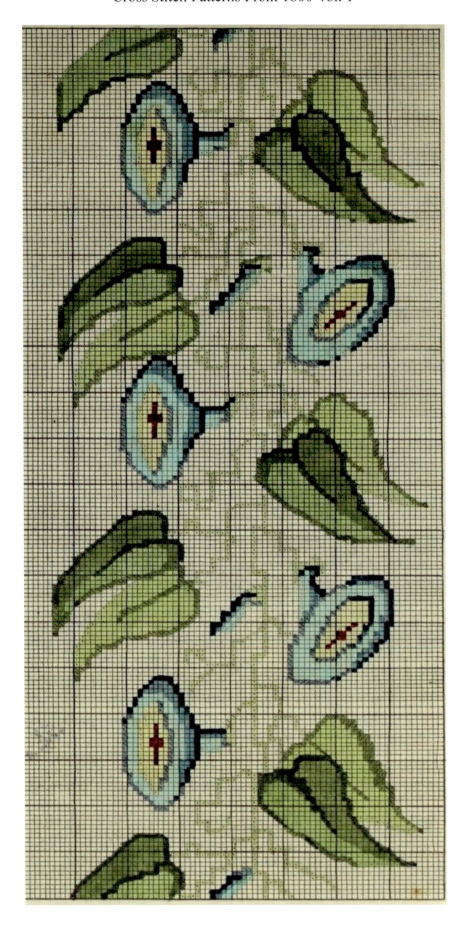

Cross Stitch Patterns From 1800 Vol. 1

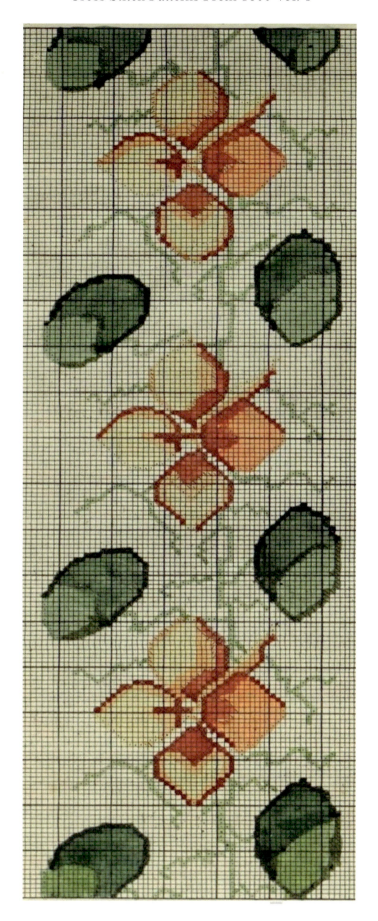

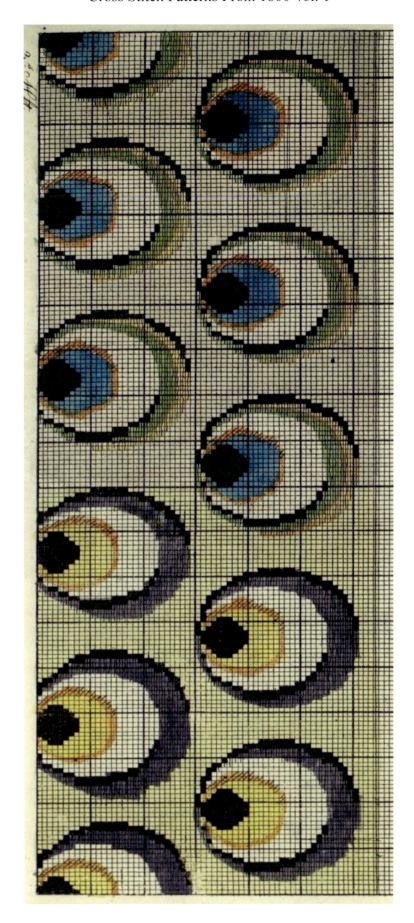

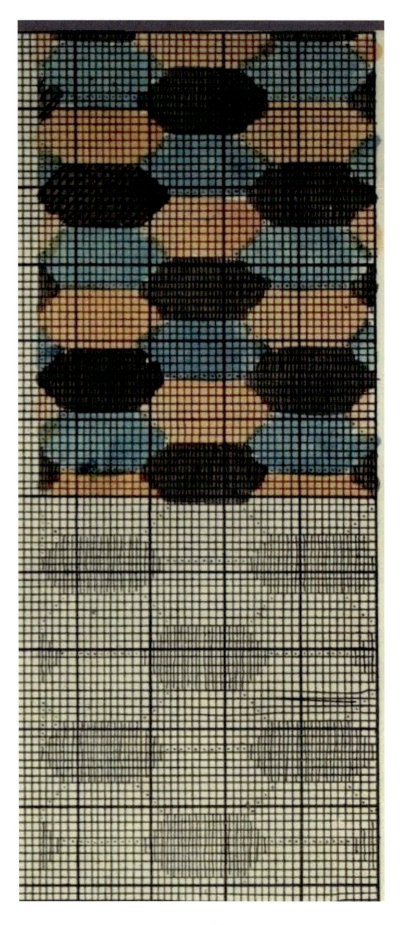

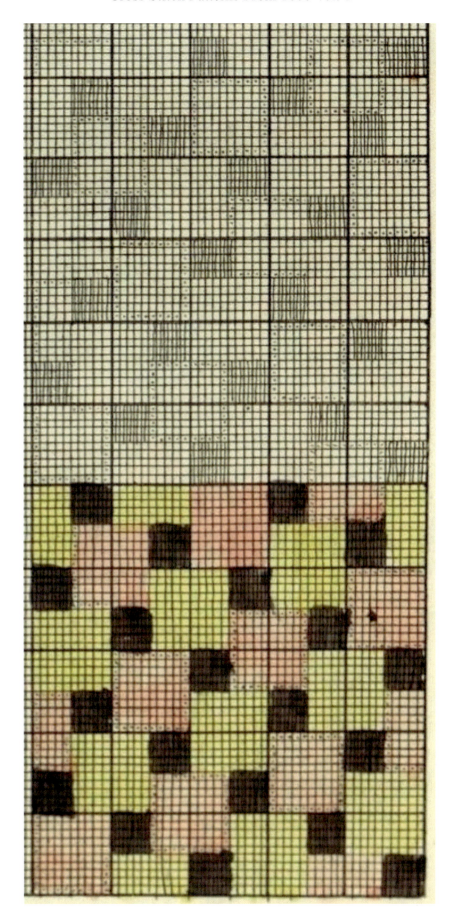

Cross Stitch Patterns From 1800 Vol. 1

Cross Stitch Patterns From 1800 Vol. 1

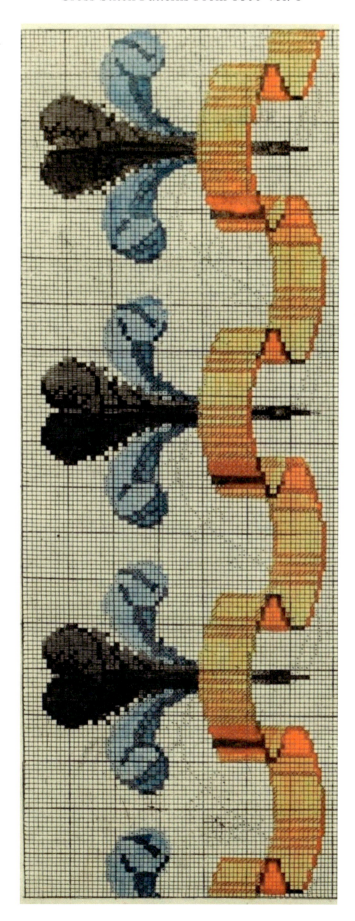

~ page 21 ~

Cross Stitch Patterns From 1800 Vol. 1

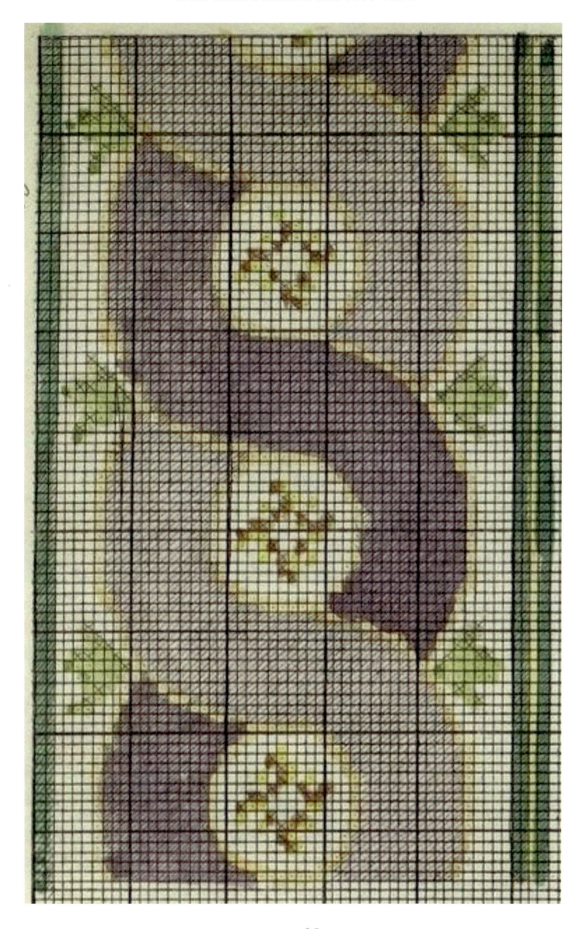

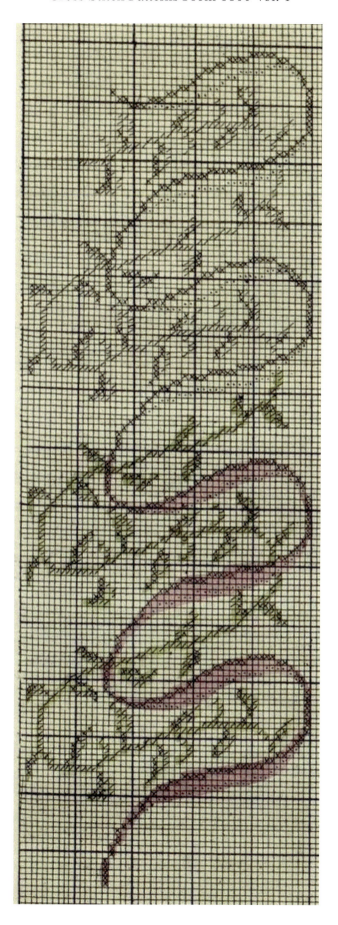

Cross Stitch Patterns From 1800 Vol. 1

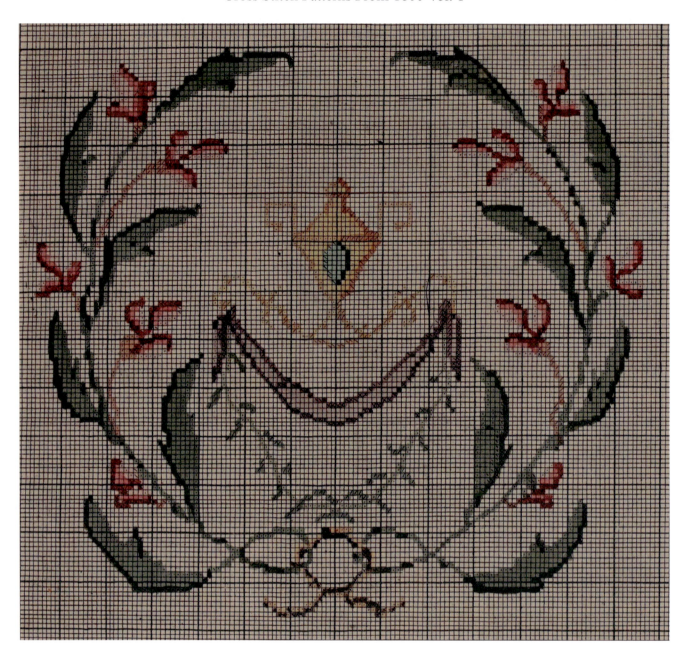

Cross Stitch Patterns From 1800 Vol. 1

Cross Stitch Patterns From 1800 Vol. 1

Cross Stitch Patterns From 1800 Vol. 1

Made in United States
Troutdale, OR
12/19/2023